Fly Fishing Flies Coloring book

Copyright Notice

No part of this document may be
reproduced in any form or by
any means without permission
in writing from:

Andy Steer

© 2016

info@anglingknots.com

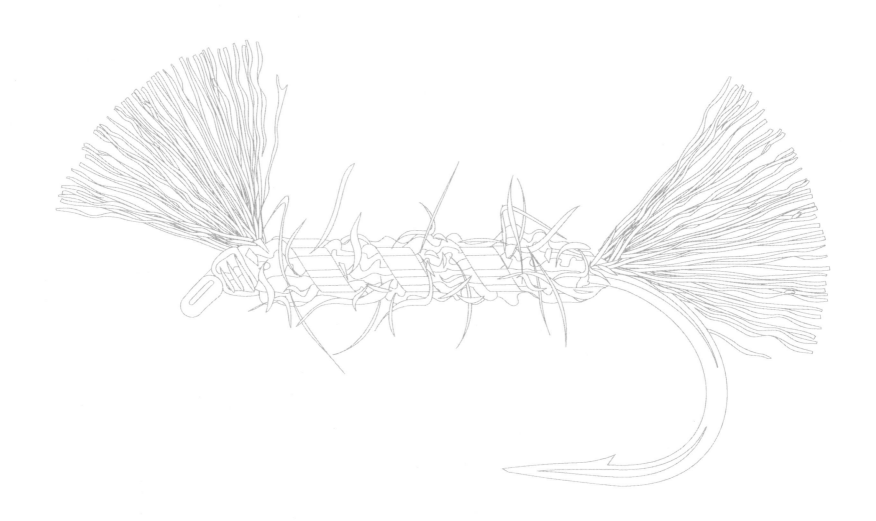

SHIPMANS BUZZER

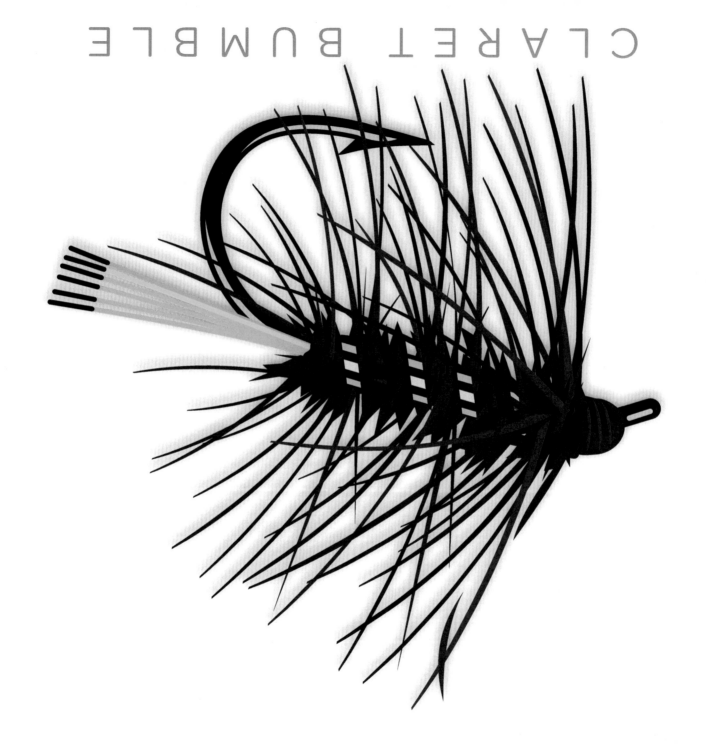

CLARET BUMBLE

SOLDIER PALMER

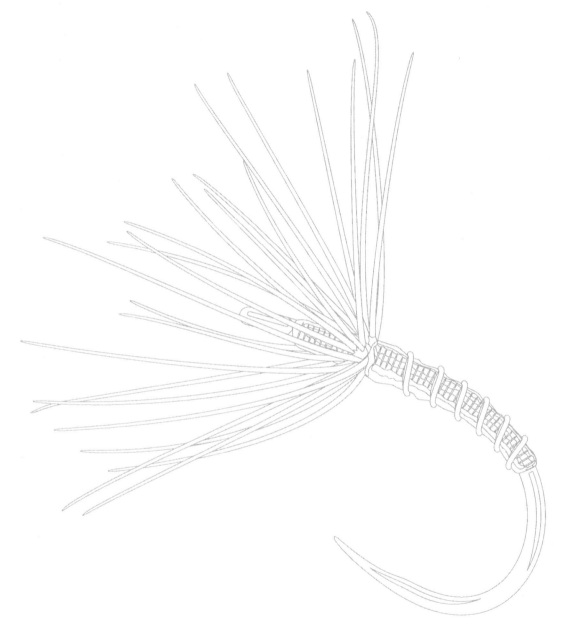

SAKASA KEBARI

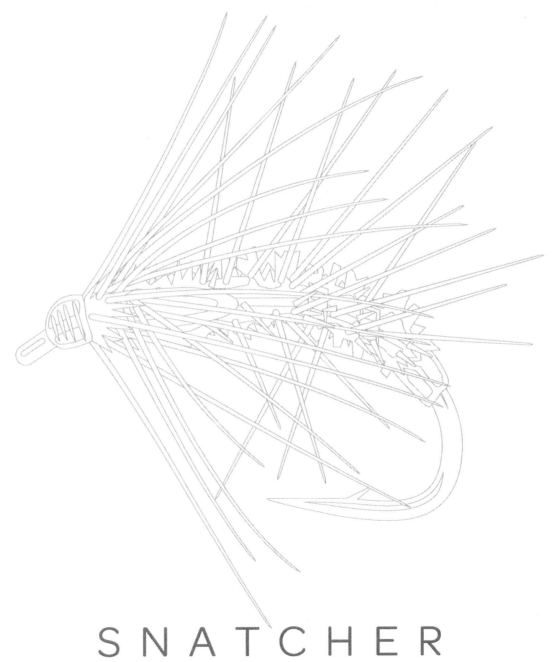

SNATCHER

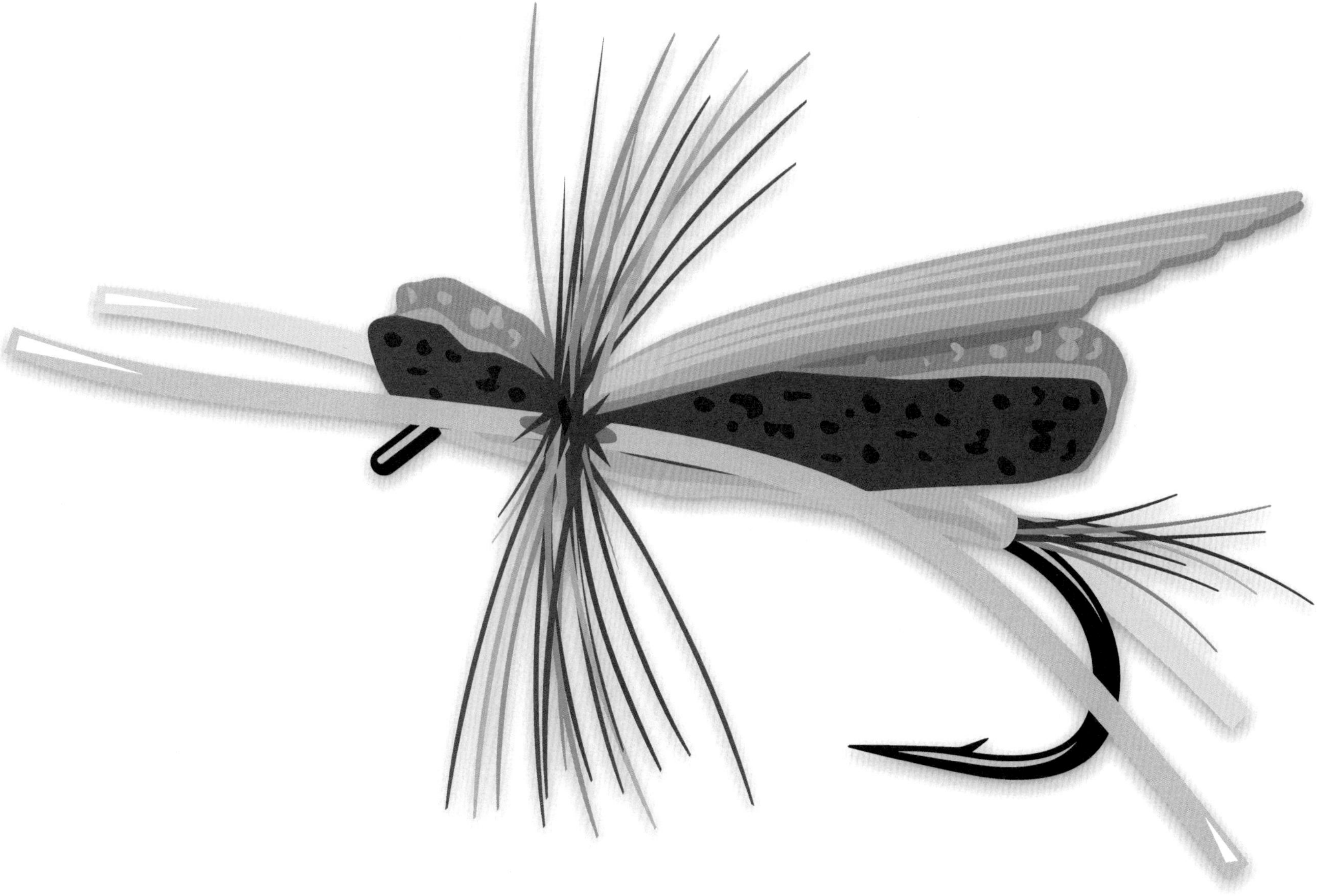

FOAM HOPPER

FOAM HOPPER

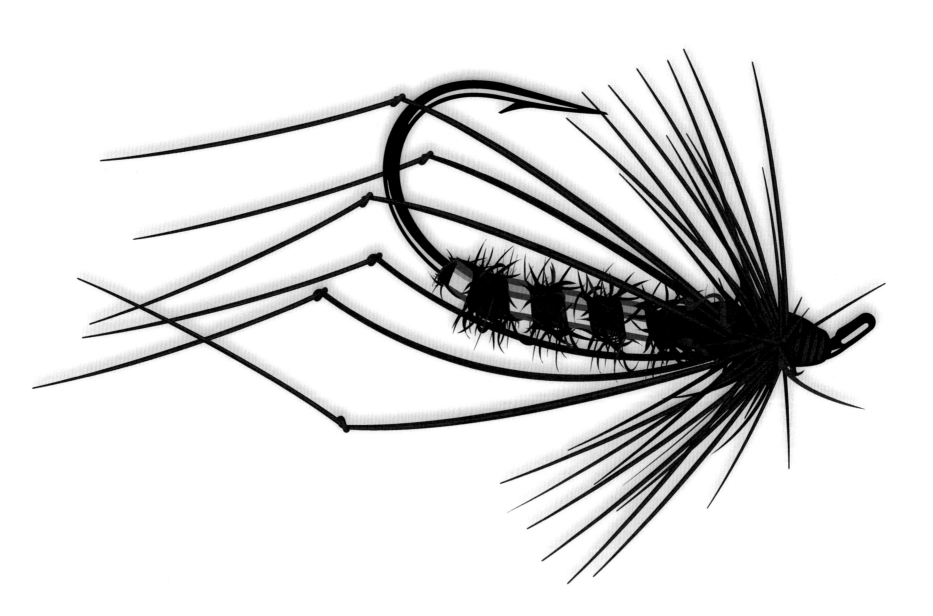

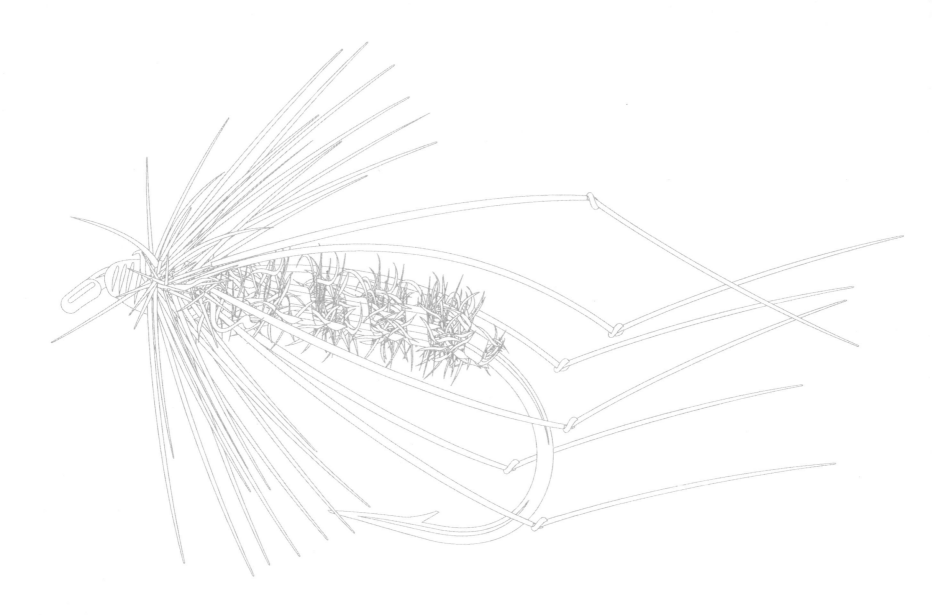

CLARET HOPPER

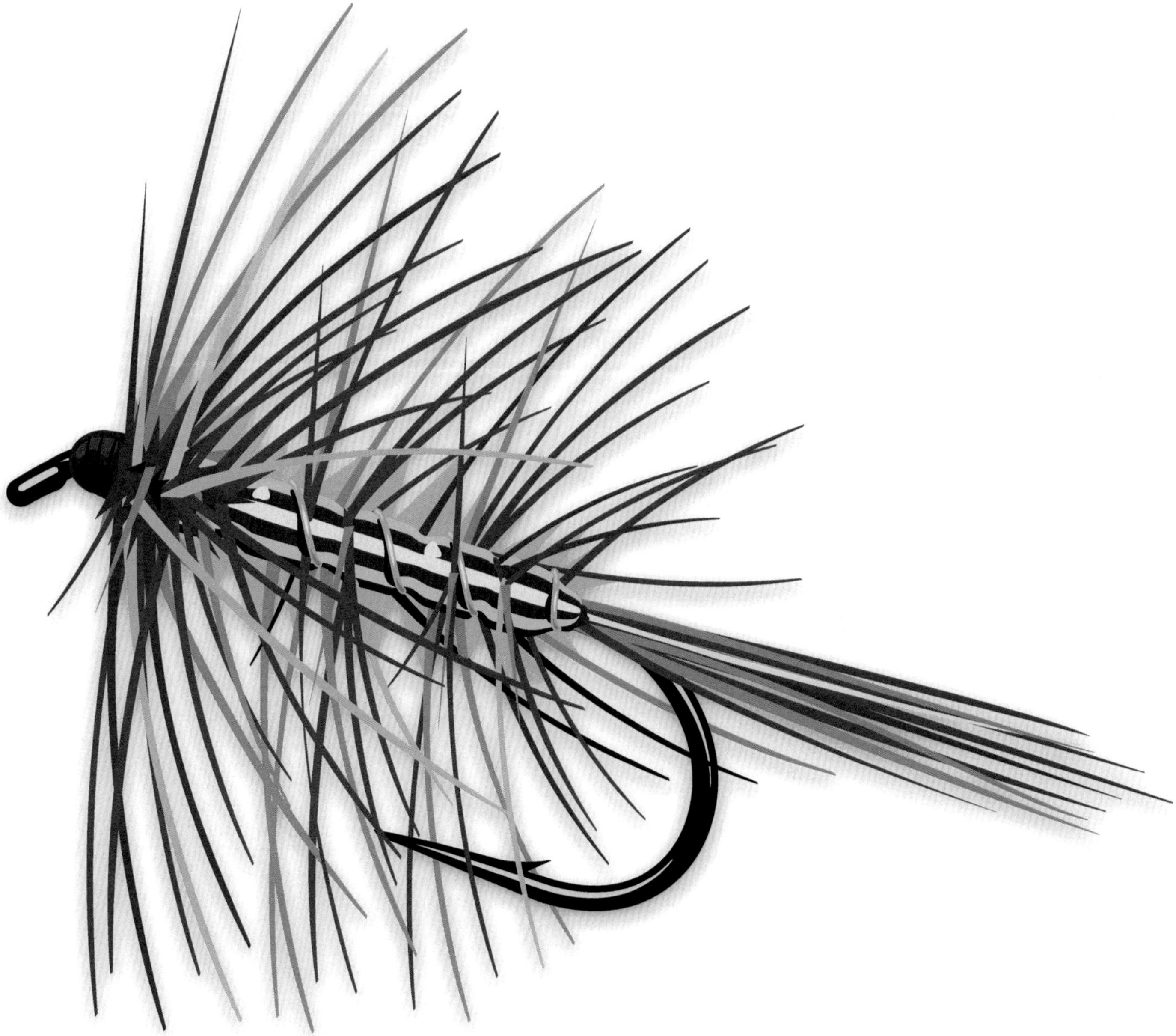

WINGLESS WICKHAM

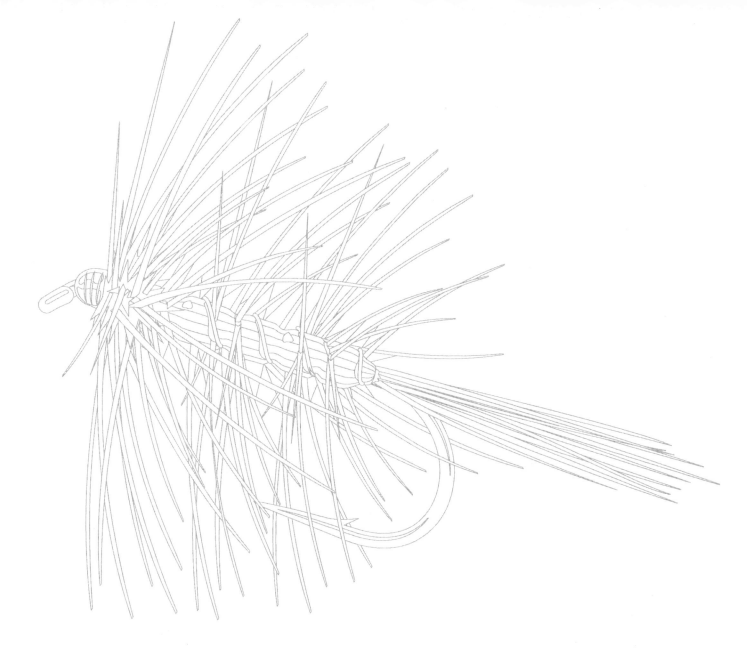

WINGLESS WICKHAM

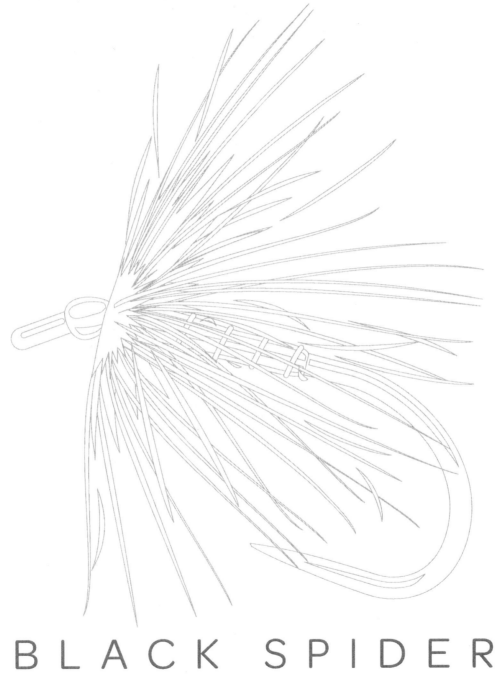

BLACK SPIDER

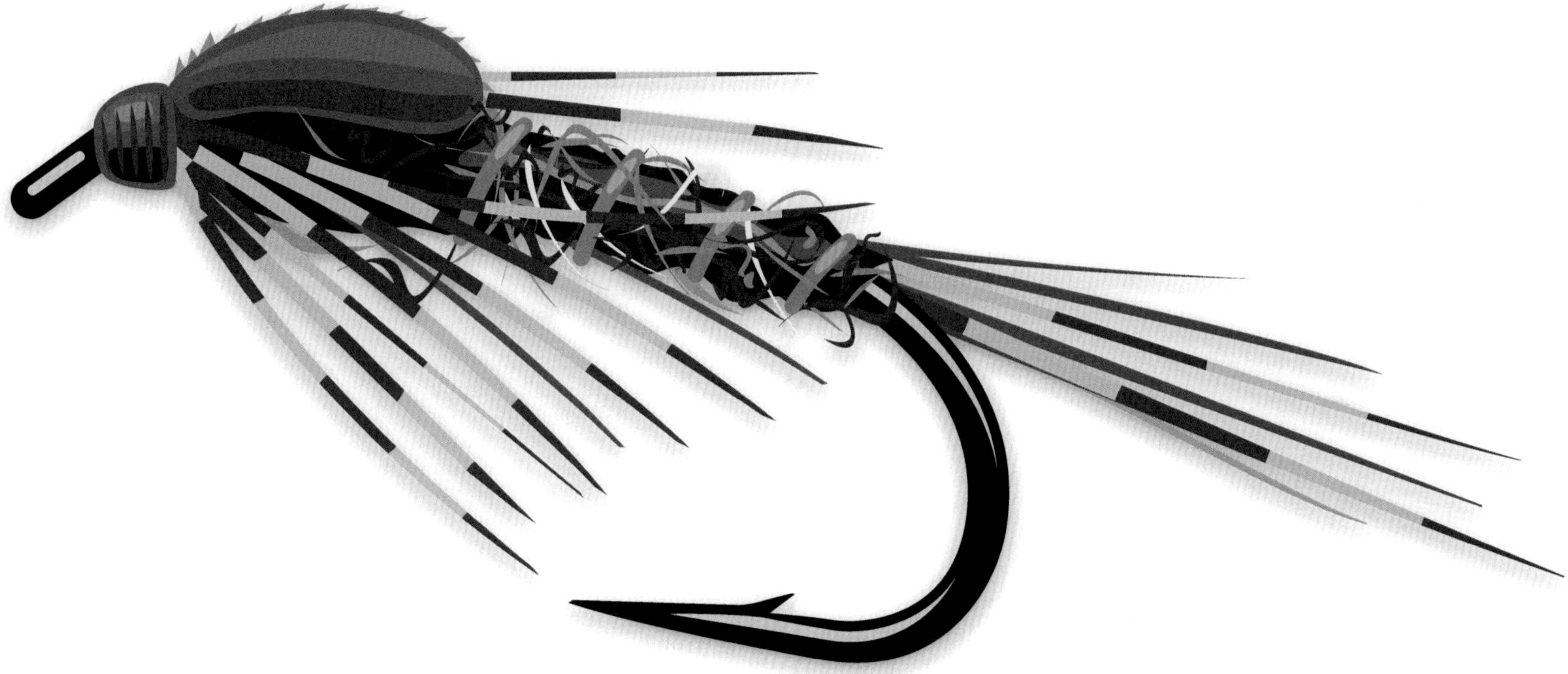

BAETIS EMERGER

BAETIS EMERGER

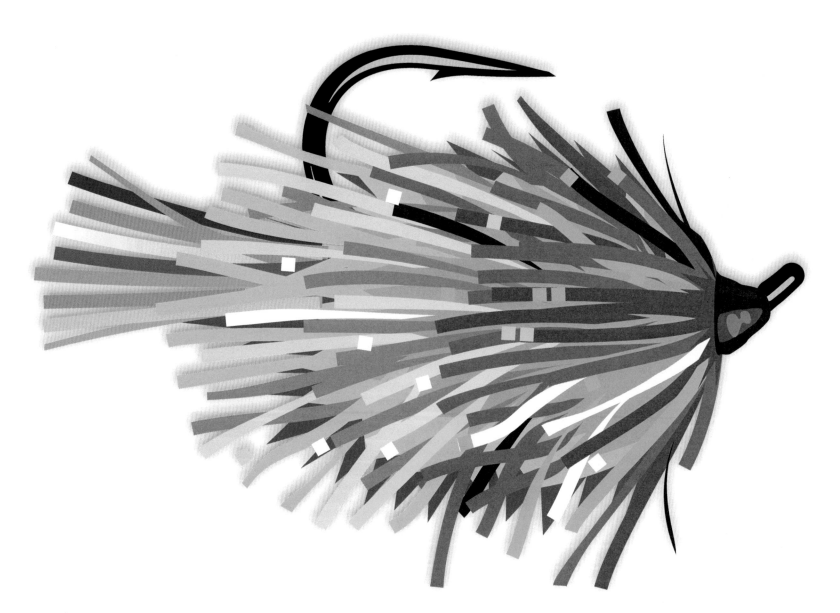

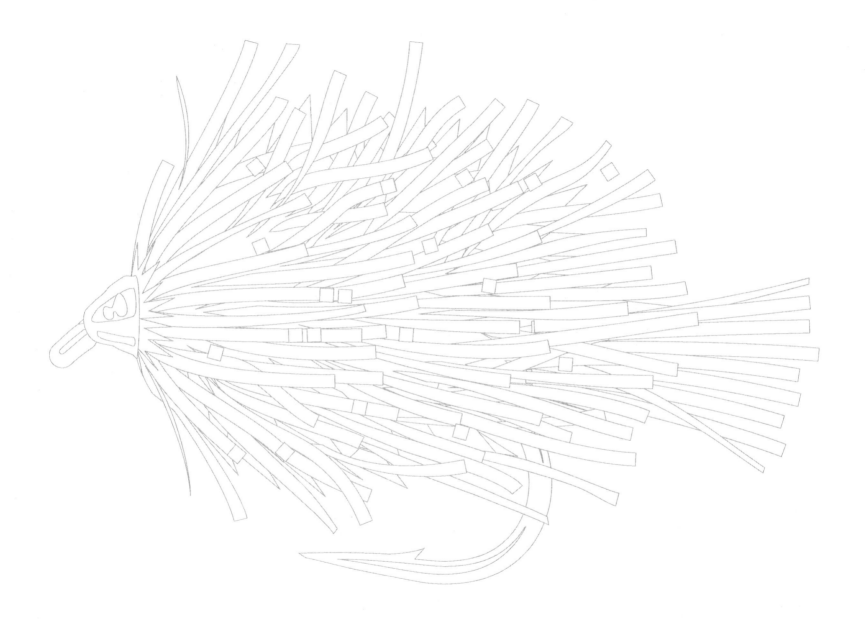

TEQUILA BLOB

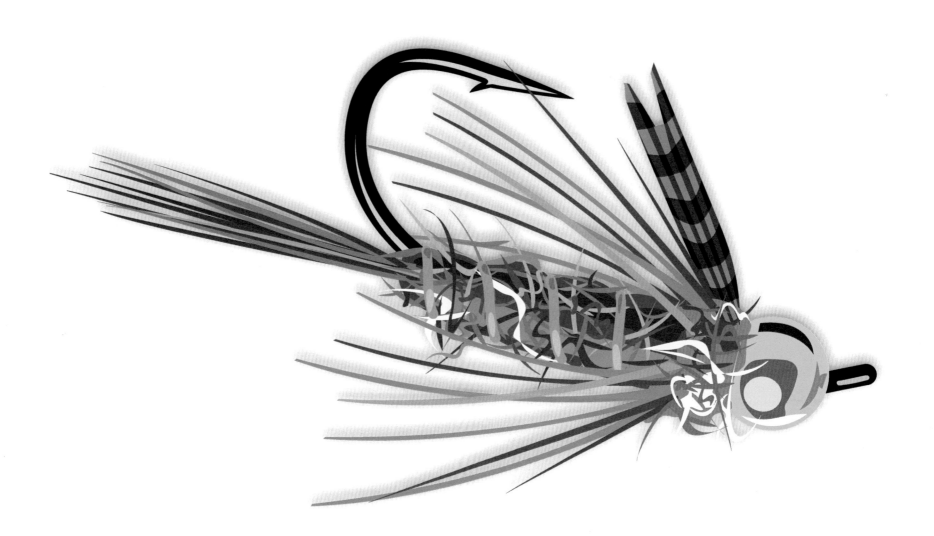

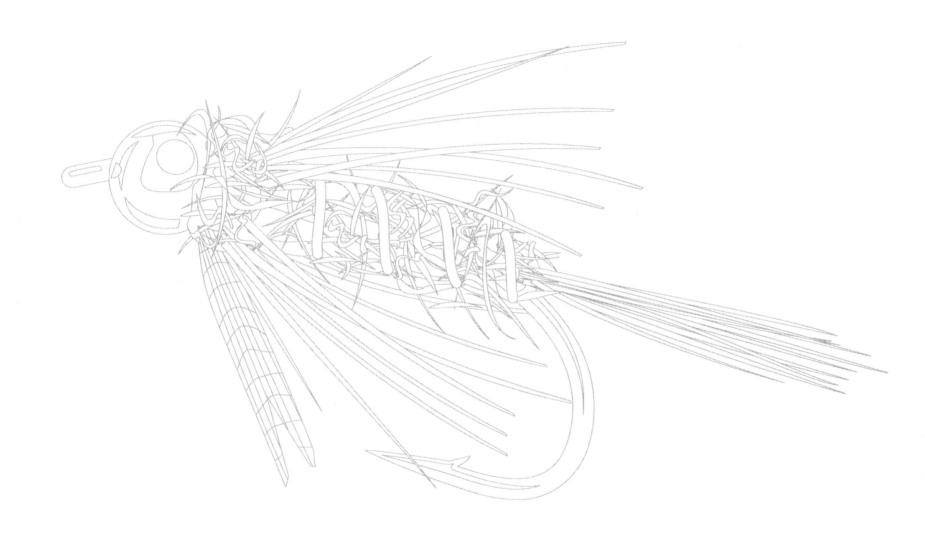

ALDER NYMPH

KATE MCLAREN

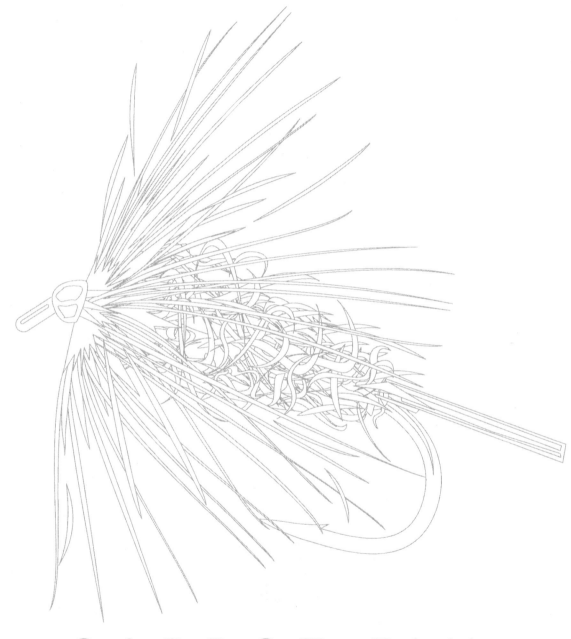

CARROT FLY

INVICTA

VIVA

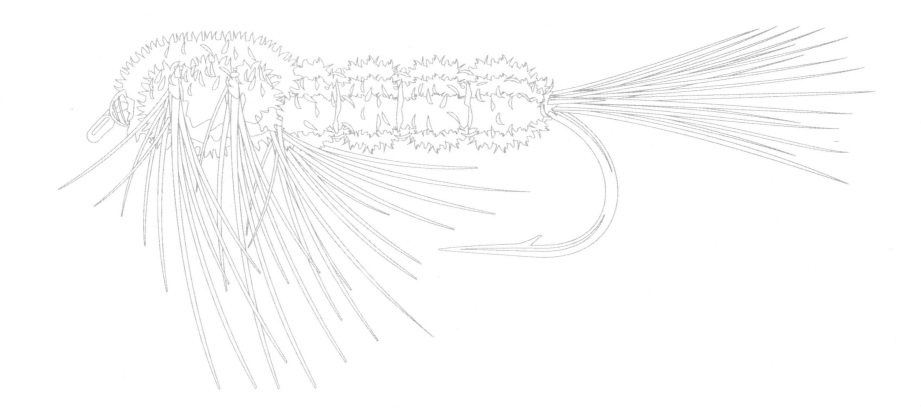

MONTANA

MINKIE

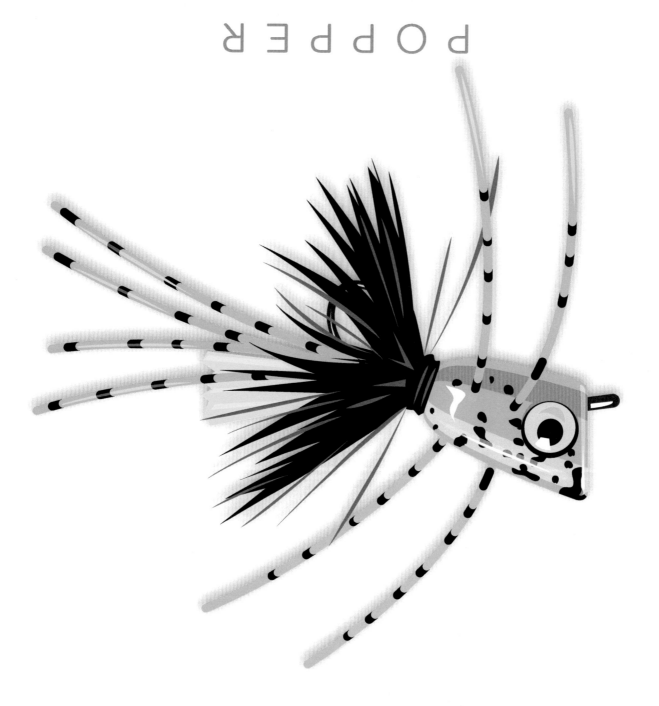

POPPER

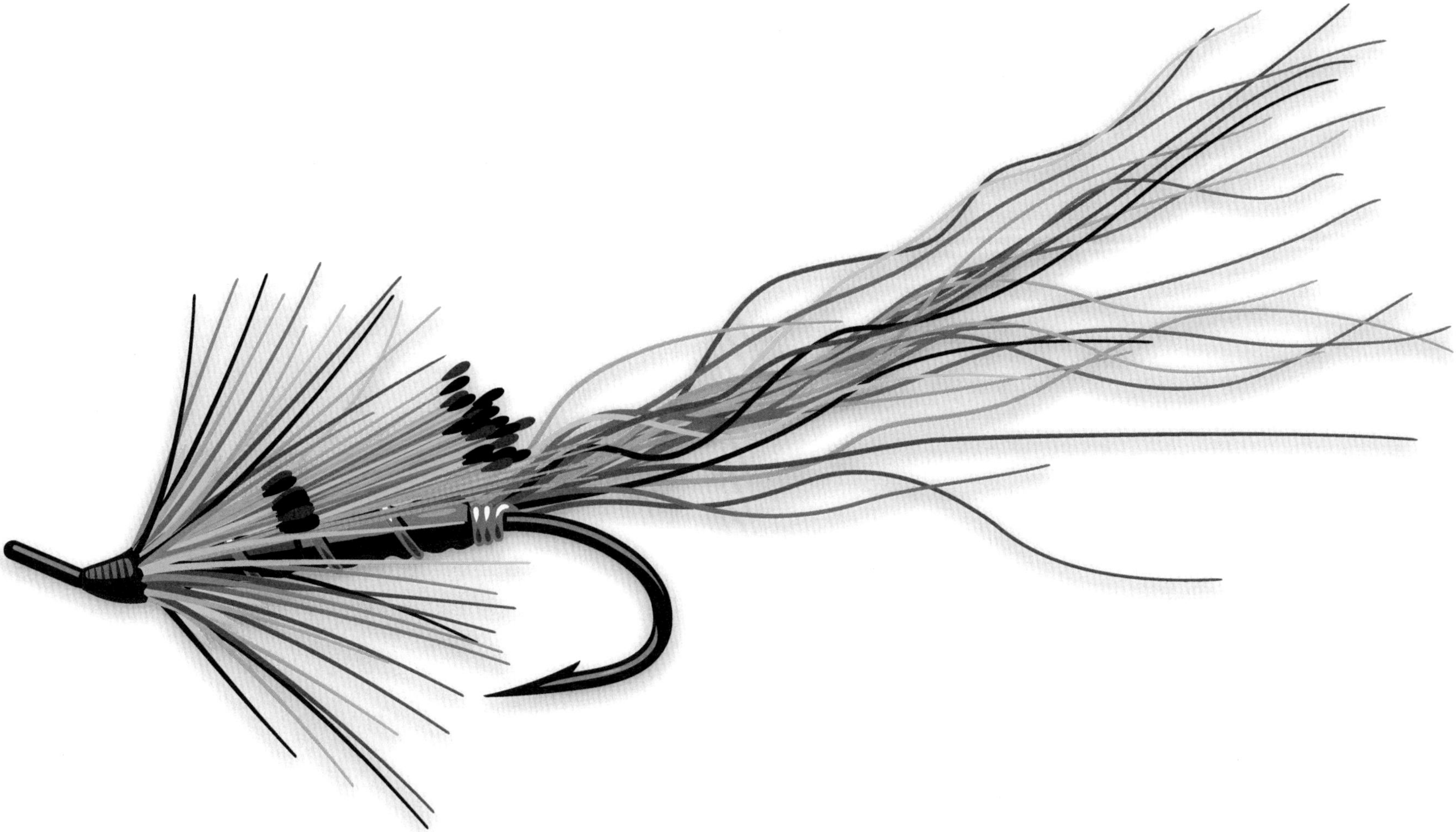

ALLY'S SHRIMP

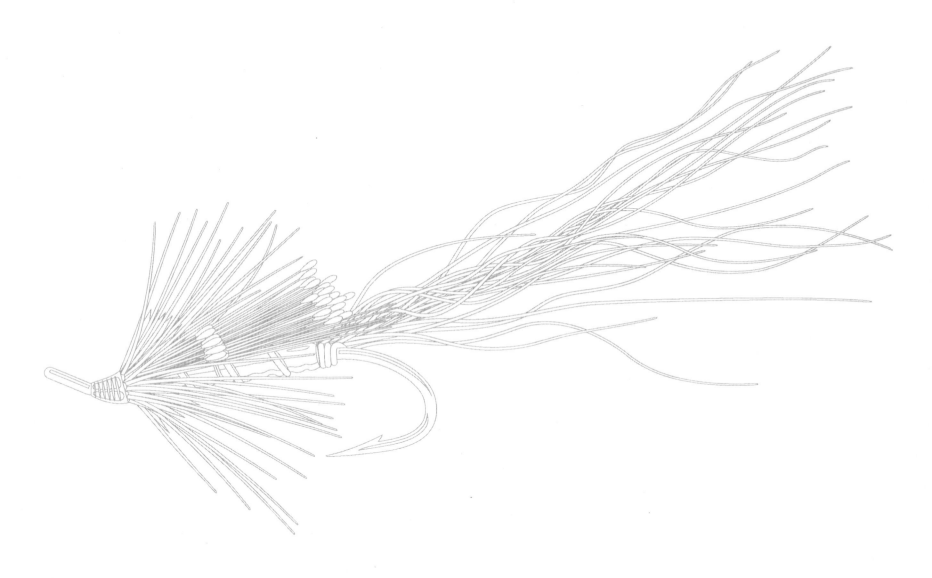

ALLY'S SHRIMP

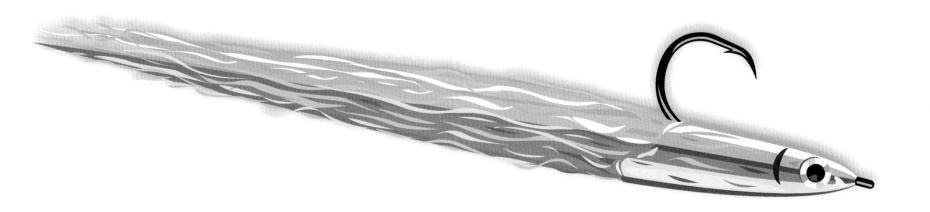

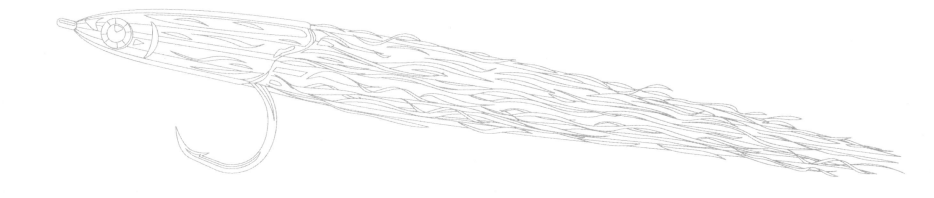

SURF CANDY

BONEFISH SPECIAL

© Andy Steer

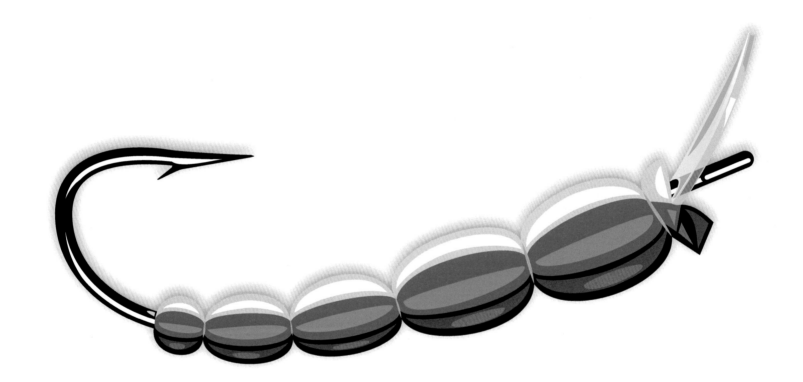

MARTIE'S WOBBLE FLY

The flies included in this 1st edition are:

Shipmans Buzzer	Kate McLaren
Claret Bumble	Carrot Fly
Soldier Palmer	Invicta
Sakasa Kebari	Viva
Snatcher	Montana
Foam Hopper	Minkie
Claret Hopper	Popper
Wingless Wickham	Ally's Shrimp
Black Spider	Surf Candy
Baetis Emerger	Bonefish Special
Tequila Blob	Martie's Wobble Fly
Alder Nymph	

Your feedback is appreciated,
so any comments or suggestions are welcome.
info@anglingknots.com

Made in the USA
Middletown, DE
26 November 2017

53267708R00029